The Boning Hall

MARY O'MALLEY was born in Connemara and educated at University College, Galway. Her previous collections of poetry include *A Consideration of Silk* (1990), *Where the Rocks Float* (1993), *The Knife in the Wave* (1997) and *Asylum Road* (2001). She has completed residencies in both Derry and Mayo, taught writing in prison, schools and universities, and edited two books of children's writing and *The Waterside Book* from her time in Derry.

GW00359570

Also by Mary O'Malley

MARY O'MALLEY

The Boning Hall

New and Selected Poems

CARCANET

First published in Great Britain in 2002 by
Carcanet Press Limited
4th Floor, Conavon Court
12–16 Blackfriars Street
Manchester M3 5BQ

A CIP catalogue record for this book
is available from the British Library

ISBN 1 85754 598 2

The publisher acknowledges financial assistance
from the Arts Council of England

Set in Monotype Garamond by XL Publishing Services, Tiverton
Printed and bound in England by SRP Ltd, Exeter

For my children

Dark one are you restless…
            Thomas Kinsella. From 'The Táin'.

But here in the Advent-darkened room
        … we'll return to Doom
The knowledge we stole but could not use.
                    Patrick Kavanagh

Acknowledgements

I would like to thank Jessie Lendennie of Salmon Press, who published the collections from which the selections in this volume are taken, and Christy Moore for the title. Some of these poems have previously appeared in the following publications: *Shenandoah*, *The Recorder*, *New Hibernia Review*, *The Shop* and *The Irish Times*.

M O'M

Contents

New Poems

New Poems

Pegeen Mike's Farewell to the Playboy

The strand is white, the tide is out,
the last ferry has pulled away from the pier.
Below a line of council houses
a red scarf lies on the sand,
a wound fading at the edges.
This is where the knife stabbed the island
again and again and again.

A breeze plays softly with skin.
A young bull roars out of memory, cut.
A timber-ended tourniquet
clips the absence off neatly.
The wind stirs the silk, fingers
the scarf, picks it up. It struts
across the limestone catwalk.

You were looking for one red image –
just a streak to relieve the grey.
You thought there were only the haws,
poison berries, a swish of fuchsia. Here, love,
adventure is not playacting. The dark man
takes his place by right.
When night falls, blades flash.

The Boning Hall

... *the wreck and not the story of the wreck*
the thing itself and not the myth ...

Adrienne Rich

No one goes diving into coffin ships but if they did
with the desire for pearls quelled they'd see wonders:
limbs streaming by, the rush of blood, oxygen, water,
bubbling with the slipstream. Then the flesh stripped
to the bones, flensed and the master saying 'measure twice,
cut once, the same for a steel boat as a set of pipes.'

Bone pipes. A phosphorescent shape, not fish,
not seal-woman but essence, slips
through the eye of a needle, of a storm
past the fabulous galleons, the gold coin,
down to where the black water is
and the little open-mouthed bone-harp sings
not of the names for things you cannot say
but the long round call of the thing itself.

Fairy Tale

And so we move into the cold,
the sufficing indifference,
the 'We know how that goes' of those
who have given up; or try to save ourselves
with a cool lie. The mind plays over us
finds you pitiful, me ridiculous.
Its blue light fingers cracks, ugly fissures.

None of it will do. I hear the echo of your laugh
bouncing off the rockface near the ledge
where you fitted every inch of your body to mine,
where we prayed love would be enough,
that you could save me from the dead
stalking the plains. Because for a while
we wanted this more than all our joined minds
could see, we wandered on until the last page.
where we cuddled together in the dark woods
of what we knew, and stroked and whispered
until daybreak when we slept and were afraid.

The Art of House Maintenance

He bought a house, stripped it to the bedrock, then began
rebuilding in his own image, putting himself together
over the rubble of marriages, lovers, occasional children.
He consulted her on each phase, the shape of a table – round;
the floors, pale wood; the walls, all white. She advised
colour. He refused. I lived next door. The house filled with light.

The death-light of the inland north kills shadows.
She would have known the signs with drink or dirty pictures.
By the time he unpacked the complete Carl Jung and the I Ching
she was trapped. She crouched. The house became a tabernacle
to keep her in. Emanations of white drove him to excess –
clean, he said, so clean. Spilled tea was a catastrophe.

She ran away. In Lisbon the colours are laid on thick.
Sienna and ochre powdered her skin, aboriginal dust.
The stone mosaic is satin underfoot. It was bright, hot. She dived,
swam, remembered when grey was the only colour –
cardigans, ratskin boots. Then revolution, the intimate squares
across which red carnations surged, joyous as victory or blood.

Back in her own place, she lies half drowned. I live upstairs.
On St Brigid's day she stirs. Her womb is cold.
She lights the sacred heart lamp and faces the empty rooms
without the liberated glow a therapist depends on.
Her need is naked and past its prime. Spring
he'd say, promise. Her hope rises like work to be done.

The Ice Age

Here we are after the real winter.
It froze so deep that the meltwater

runs thick with old debris – knotted wool
the devil in a dream. The well-executed heel

of a sock turned on its mathematically elegant
point follows the shavings from slats soaked for months

in a turlough that appeared below the home house
every water-logged November. Now your drawings,

films, darkroom equipment – all this murk
coming downriver makes no sense. The stark

truth seems to be that we are ourselves stuck
among things that will not float yet, artefacts

of the constructed life, its seams unravelled.
This morning Kathleen Ferrier is singing Mahler

'Nun seh ich wohl …' … I have no German.
The mantelpiece floats past. Our photographs are sliding.

The thaw burns. It has been twenty-two years. Cleave,
I think. Cleft. The words pitch like holed vows.

Poem for my Birthday

This is between you and me alone Mother.
I have never liked those fleshy poems
wet milk and birthslime, the baby urgent, then content.
I was no easy infant, cramped, mewled, howled.
I was a scrawny crow, a scaltán, never satisfied.

This is between you and me, Mother.
What right have I now?
You never had time for my crowtalk
the melodeon squawks and fiddle screeches
the odd sweet note I hit
saying oh look – the gaoled fire dancing,
are those stripy things tigers or nuns?
The water running away, running river
the rain-red fox after the hens.
And a pain here where that scrapy thing
is missing from my chest, then a rusty howl
but still, mother, what right have I to ask
and what, as the other women of the Pleiades say
would be the point?

Prescribing the Pill

Say goodbye to the fixed idea:
a mother holding a child
looking at it in the appraising way
you would a treasured ring,
an emerald or a wedding band
with becoming pride, muted joy.

Say goodbye to that idea.
Get rid of it as if it were
a straining dog's leash
a primed shotgun.
People always say 'Let it go'
as if it were that simple
but there's recoil.

This mother has no choice.
All her life she has loved the sea, a man, hills.
Now this, the serpent coiled in her ovary.
Its black lidless eyes look out through hers
every time she makes love
and there will always be more of them.

She knows she has been blessed.
A man's lips on the underside of her wrist
his body guarding her back
led to this. She loves all her children
but this one. It is the idea's fault
and she has clutched this idea close –
see how her eyes guard it.

She's due to be churched.
The baby knows nothing of this
but all her life a hunger for cobalt blue
will course through her belly like a rip-tide.

'My role was that of an observer'

General Robert Ford

Your blue eyes, Danny boy,
your black hair.

They were all armed, the men. Marching!
And that shape there is ...
Very like a gun.
No, more like a nailbomb, forsooth.
Yes, your honour, very like a nail bomb.
More like a widget, methinks, m'lord. Yes
very like a widget, so we shot it.
Widgety Lord Widgery. Thirteen widgets
weapon carriers, every seventeen-year-old
Fenian one of them, Sir.

It was a Sunday. There was snow.
Thirty years ago. Seventeen
the age to love, the year to die.
Your dark hair, Danny boy,
your blue terrorist eyes.

Solo

Woken from a dream of cold water
my skin calls for it.
You will get up, light a fire, make coffee.
Then your bare feet on the stairs.
Dawn crosshatches the bed.
Beyond the window
fat little sheep are lit like candles.

I slip in beside you, taste the coffee
on your tongue
walk down my own bare stairs
while the house is sleeping. This morning
I do not understand timing,
geography, the way lives slide
down under the backs of cushions.

The Ballad of Caitlin and Sean*

i.m. Michael Hartnett

His hands explored her rounded hills,
the mounds and underground passages.
He was here to discover on this journey
a country he could love like no other. Never
like this before, even with India. He mapped her,
would have planted her but this was Connaught.

For a while she was his border country
the boats, the guns, his brush with wildness.
She was his destiny, he said, so Irish with her temper
such a woman, with her hysterics and demands
for repeal. He loved and understood her
as he never had his home counties. She said,

'That's what they all say,' but loved his hands,
his faith in maps, the shine and glint
of astrolabe and compass. She whispered,
'My love you will betray me like all your kind
but be for a time my safe house.'
Because his bedtime stories brought rest

from the poison and sweetness of her own language
she relished English, the bladed consonants of his love.
The vowels that bubbled out of his mouth
like glass beads, so perfectly oval, are the real reason
why after all these years
she teaches his bastards their shamed lineage.

---

* Caitlin Ní hUallacháin and John Bull.

Seascape, Errislanann

For D.J.H.

Light streaked off the water. The wind rose.
You found a sea urchin above the breakers
still whole, thrown up on the round stones,
'Protected by the form of the sphere I suppose.'

Back at the house, exhilarated and salty
over coffee and treacherous amaretti
you handed me a pretty toy or case
powder compact size but thicker – the wheel
of a toy tractor perhaps, café au lait
but they come in ice-blue and rose.
I guessed twice and gave up, amused.

'It's an anti-personnel device. They float in
on the tide. Children like them.' You sketched
the severed leg, tendons, how the damage
to someone small is higher up. Accident and design.
'This one's Italian like your shoes.
Some factory outside Milan makes them.'

There are times when the world empties of sound.
When you said, 'Disarmed, of course,' and smiled
the tight skin on my hand tasted almonds. Then the rush
of wind falling, the words' backthrust.

September Twelfth

Alive? Well? Working
down the dark slide
into the underworld
where a guide
whispers warnings,
the dragons' teeth are seeding:
three mirrors to the night sky
my only protection.

Persephone Astray

'... I've always kept a unicorn
and I never sing out of tune ...'
Sandy Denny

At solstice I slide deep into it, up for it this once,
choice, chance, downfall, the inevitable winter vortex.
In a stone tower near the shops, the cards.
The reader is motherly. She lays them out.
In the centre, malevolent goat's head
red body packed tight, grin like toothy fruit
a helix of sprung life from eyes to sex
the king of hell pirouettes like a TV presenter.

Lifting him, she revealed a card of sun or stars.
He proffers wrinkled fruit. Something stirs in me.
My eyes rake the deck for swords.
It's time to go dealing. My hands burn across the cards.
I make three cuts. I will meet him halfway
be what he made me, queen of the dead.
'It's time to get rid of him. He blocks the light.'
The reader's eyes are Chagall blue.

I'll be his mirror, the foxed surface spread like skin
or painted on, watery, stagnant, the sky silvered
with lake light, the bog sucking me in
but don't make me leave him
in the shade of his own terrible mother.
I'll tumble-the-wildcat if that's what it takes
but this time I want him with me, my six months' dark side
when I surface into the pale wash of March.

'He renegued before and got you by trickery.
Now you want to bring him home and have fun.
The cold wind will wither your skin.
Do you think your mother bargained for nothing?
It can be done. A breath let out, the graded sink
the space between the hips turning to ballast.
The body rests in lotus on the bottom. Then panic, flight
upwards propelled by the lungs straining.

Pearl fishers know the best training
and sponge divers. Ask them. Teach the mind
to overcome instinct.' Live in the intellect's light
accurate and harsh as middle-aged lines?
Alright. I'll go down with the gloomy bastard again
and come up on my own but I want to smuggle in
great cataracts of Spanish sun. Stella, he called me. Stella.
Now his red star will go out but the crops will ripen.

The Crow on the Cradle

After Onassis married Jaqueline
a woman able to stay thin
the distraught Callas alone in Paris
laboured down the sprung arpeggios
she had slipped up light as sin.
She descended into Tosca, the walled garden.

Against Jackie's Frenchified elegance,
her remote smile, Maria's silence shouted.
She bowed out badly, all tantrums,
star of her own little opera.
The notes – just too blue – treacled
and the air turned viscous.
On records the voice is blood and honey. Listen.
She's praying to the moon, dying for a man.

Billie

Men just loved Billie.
Her unblaming pain
made them want to hurt her more
just to hear that voice soar and dip,
the little rasp, silk on a nail file, as it slid
up from her belly.

Star of the Sea

You were the cut glass pilgrimage
the reek I climbed up and down, not always
on my knees. You were a shadow in the cup
but your hard aging body held its shape.

Briefly, but long enough to lead me
in and out of a dark valley and long enough
for the small worm of cancer in your dreams
to infect every sleep – no love can cure this.

I reached the shrine you made, where you vowed
to be mine, adored my image with incense.
In the picture I have a necklace of sea and am happy.
I remember the day – you were beside me.

This sweet adoration exposed my heart.
A voice whispered 'I am the Lord thy God ...'
I fled for good, then walked barefoot on glass
to get back to you. Droplets of blood jewelled the snow.

They would. The soles of the feet remember sin
and flinch but set down firmly and walk on
knowing pain numbs and is sweet, that paradise
awaits, or at least a respite from hell. For reward, a vision.

I saw the sun spin, slowly at first. Then
under my feet the light. Splintering.

Rebuilding the St John

The fire is lit in a ring of rough stones
on which a gas drum sits crookedly.

It hisses steam through a long pipe
into a chamber where the planks

are urged into the curves that make
a boat female and pliant. Her skeleton

is strong, wide-haunched and thick-ribbed,
the bow cleaved deep as a horse's chest.

In a plastic tent the builder is adding length
to the mast – pennies for luck, or to pay Charon

will be placed under it. They are re-building
the St John closer to Homer's specifications

than Brussels'. This is no postcard, it is a place,
a boatyard where craftsmen use what is to hand

to follow patterns handed down, inscribed
on the sand at low tide, measured out in the sea's sound.

Here tradition decrees there will be fire in a boat,
the new rules broken, the old laws kept.

PMT – The Movie

It arrives a day early for once, bloody but unbowed,
living proof that God's a man. Taken by surprise again
Diana wonders whether Actaeon might have been
better left to his gazing, after all those breasts were full
and with the water splashing, the way the sun slanted
in the groves would make Sam Goldwyn hire
the lighting technician.

                         This happened every month
and you'd think, she said to her nymphs,
a goddess would know if the rage that whirled through her
like a ninja and attacked whoever crossed her path
was cyclical and came from the swollen place between
her hips. Tell that to your CAT scan, she told the gynaecologist.
I feel it comes from the red hot centre of my brain
and I'm listening to my instincts.

                       The nymphs agreed,
had the same problem and now they were synchronised –
Actaeon had been gorgeous but day twenty-six
was not auspicious among the maidens.
Now he was just pitiful and made scary noises.
Maybe those evening primroses could have saved him,
such a pretty flower. Pity Zeus hadn't said what they were for.

The Climber

I am his last mistress, distinguished
from the casual rides, middle-of-the-night
tussles by a sentence in the biography,
mentioned because I broke ranks, cried audibly
at his funeral. I was desperate for his wildcat loving.
'No one else, ever again' ... I was young.

I'd have lost him, one way or another. For the record
he tumbled into every woman he met, stoned, wired.
That's how it was then, the men spurred one another on
the girls went along like vessels. A bit neanderthal.

When he crashed, I catapulted, wised up, pitched
my worth. After that, I met my match, had four kids.
I'm a fulfilled wife, in case anyone wonders. Look
no regrets. Only today, I opened the wrong book.

Hunting

Burn the mansion, Scarlett, watch Tara become ruin.
Build a stone house out of the increased dimensions
of the air, out of velvet-lined conversations
held nightly with the architect on the telephone.

Four rooms, one to prepare lemony food and eat,
one with a warm hearth in front of which to sit,
a room facing the mountain the first snow dusts.
This will have a gas fireplace. Then a room to work.

One to sleep. Where? The big open-windowed room
also facing the snowy mountain, or the street in a small town
or the terraced ordinary houses in some inland suburb
where bins go out on Tuesdays, and the *Telegraph* is delivered?

I'd like that now. Especially with the gauze curtains
and the skylight, undressed to look out on incarnadine clouds.

The Dinner Table

We have done what we could,
have carved our refuge out of clouds,
swapped a heart, lung, clear vision
for ruin, this grief we did not select.

There is one thing to be said – we built
these walls, hewed a house out of wind.
The hedge of escalonia you tended succeeded.
We sit here, sheltered, with the odd echo.

Dinner is ready, the table laid. There will be
no more arrivals. A salmon sits on a terracotta dish,
the salad in a swirl of glass, a final twist
of lemon on each white plate. We have no appetite.

Only the slant of pewter light, the way
your body's planes caught it, the children's
high cries snatched from a stream of play, mattered.
There is no relief in remaining. Slowly we eat.

Casida *of the one Wounded by the River*

After Lorca

The stones on the riverbed talk. They are not intimate.
The words seduce under water's sussurus
but listen to their dead flat vowels. Their dry comments
on the people by the banks have no resonance.
They rustle like dead letters.

                    Their hard little hearts
are hollow, each chamber full of stale air. A walker
stops. He hears. Not believing his ears he adds colour
in transcription. The stones clack on, some cackle. They know
he will turn even this into a song for Death, his lover.

The Escape

It seemed easy. She travelled across Ireland by train,
snow-comforted, reversing the last slow-motion

passage of 'The Dead'. Among the bare trees – a red
jacketed man, and women in fur hats – who wouldn't

think of Russia – Clara and Kildare transformed
into outposts of St Petersburg. In the city she negotiated

the frozen wastes of Grafton Street, thought
how nobody but her seemed to be leaving, bought

a large bunch of irises for the blue, their yellow
tongues. Set them in a vase to open, a bathyscope glow.

Fleeing wives everywhere do this or step
out onto the tracks. At the flat, she slept.

The irises flamed like gas jets. Sculpted heads
looked down from every nook and plinth, bored –

next day they watched her put the flowers in a plastic bag
and, carrying them carefully as you might a child

you were planning, reluctantly, to expose,
set them down by a dustbin in the snow.

A shadow hurried away, was soon gone.
She re-crossed Ireland the Joycean way, home

through the dead centre of the country in a train packed
with revellers, reeling her life silently backwards

across the bog of Allen, the Shannon, the snow falling
still and in the churchyard, a grave. Shivering

with cold she went home, made the bed. As she watched
another New Year's Eve cemented in she wondered

if Nora had tired of being his West, if when she left
and said, 'I wish you'd go and drown yourself,' she meant it.

Polemic

When you posit a shifting Universe
rely on this – if you betray me
I will not give you one soft word
before I walk away and when you die
I will put dead flowers on your grave.

The Man of Aran

But what if it were not epic.

Before the echo sounder was invented
fishermen let down weighted piano wire,
they listened for a school to hit, a note to sound.

Perhaps a scale – grace notes as single fish
hit E flat minor, say, or strange tunes
as a shoal crescendoed through the water,
minnows and sharks, sharps and flats –
heard from above at a different pitch
not perfect, but accurate, close enough for jazz;

Their watery playing gave them up to slaughter
but the boatman dreamed of women singing
and the song coaxed him as he lured mackerel
with feathers that darted like blue jays
through the clear sea. He stayed out too long.

Let's leave it at that.
There would be cliffs rearing soon enough,
weather fighting.
No need for all that hauling of wrack
to the wrong side of the island,
for half drowning the locals, for shark.

We know how it works.
A pretty lure, hunger, the hook. No storm is as sweet
or deadly as the sting, the barb's sink.

Divorce Referendum

The house they built was solid
enough for ten generations.
It resembled a child's drawing
with an azure door, crayon smoke
curling from the chimney.

When their love boils over
it hums like a reactor.
If one of them calls the peelers
there will be law and ructions
but the house will survive, and sell.

At night when they lock up
she sees blackened walls, the door
splintered, their few sticks
out in the rain – a blue goblet
has escaped the rough handling.

Filling the dishwasher she resolves
to snap out of this. Later, he kisses her breast
and wonders if across the country,
in every republic of the heart,
couples are preparing for eviction;

deciding who is the landlord of their love,
who the croppy, and weighing the cost
against the size and colour of the sun
each child, according to his nature
has drawn above the right hand gable.

Bean Sidhe

She wants you for herself,
will have you, even as your lips
rasp a line across my hips.
When your mouth
whispers its open invocation
it is she who takes it in,
the swell of womb, wound, oh ...
she will bleed me dry,
take your seed into her, grow
ripe. I see her cold green eyes
narrow as you enter me. Jealous.
I do not fear sleep in your arms:
I can not win. She will take the words
out of your dead mouth.

The Poetry Harlots

From the Irish

They're the neo-classical can-can girls
who do not terribly matter,
but boys must accessorise
and off-duty they wear pearls. The girls.
They open their vowels
and sharpen their smiles
and converse in iambic pentameter.

Welsh Pastoral

i.m. R.S. Thomas

The chapels in your still valley are biblical,
the Jacob's sheep content and allegorical.

There was a honed edge in its Calvinist worship,
sad churches, empty, unused to glory.

Snow fell here. I thought of the shepherds' wives
gathered every Sunday, their cold comfort, bitten cries.

We deserve more than dead churches, envisioned pieties,
the practiced ring of near-death stories.

This laudanum-soaked place lured me, like a holy kiss
but we read through early imprints

I looked back as I walked out of your painted past.
The church shifted, it rose on a tide of Aves and Kyries.

A priest, golden robed, raised the host,
drank Spanish wine. Blood flowed through the veins

of a dead congregation. The women's eyes softened,
expecting first communion. A high bell shivered.

I left the way I came in. The serious men stared,
the sky moaned and every candle on the altar blazed.

The Widow's Prayer

He's gone for good this time, dead. I held the lyre,
just a strum couldn't do much harm.

Now all his wild animals run loose in my dreams.
I have no way with them and would only get attached
and cry when they tore one another apart. Weak.
Before long I'd recognise each animal by its predator.
For deer I'd say jaguar and a rooster's fine comb
would flash a handsome red brush across the screen.
That in turn would cause shrieking mounted people
to ride over the hill above my house, their red jackets
ridiculous. I'd think of bad films and then
where would we be? In the Scottish Highlands,
or Kerry with half of Hollywood in tow
and the government on its knees in gratitude.
If these night visitors are gifts to me
love, send out your sheepdog to round them up.

Tobar Mháire *

Even at low tide the sea sucks towards it.
Womb shaped, the earth-girls exclaim. No.
This is hard water, a jet pushes through rock

fresh as a bud. It calls the mouth down
to slake thirst, drink light. It is goat-horned.
Locked tight in its high rock, giving sweet water.

How greedy they all are. I sip, wet the nape
of my bare neck at swim-two-birds.
You dip, showing your arms' strength,

a fire-escape down which I will spiral
and lock, clasp and swing,
climbing into my strength, out of fear.

I calculate the angle of descent
to where the sea waits, its emerald set
low in the original magma. It is too oblique.

You are poised
too like a statue among the jut and jag.
I walk up the hill alone because, my love

I have done with saviours. Still
when no one was watching I blessed myself
and dropped a stone into the well's crystal heart.

* Mary's Well.

Cat Sense

After Boland

When you travel beware
of loose women at the ports;

they give you vile diseases
and ice the heart.

The women easily available on roads
are about what you'd expect.

It's up to you, of course
but love, think of us, the hurt,

the clean thrust of a sword
through a froth of roses.

From the Drug Notebooks*

The Past Conditional

Your sober postcard arrived today, so different from the fun
and devilment of those early letters. Your words reached
for my wrist across the distance, the black curves were cool
against my lips, dry ink – they say the bunting is out in Canada
for some saint's celebration. I shave syllables
off a line with the hilted knife, blood supplies colour.

Timing is all, last month would have worked
wonders, we'd have met between Boston and New York
you driving a sky-blue American car
would have swept down out of the North on a cold wind
to rescue me from the Cape Cod Summer
but what with travel and work, we keep missing one another.

So much is conditional – on bodies touching, on a voice
curling around your neck like a fox, settling
in the curve between head and shoulder.
On saying this small touch of your mind is a blue flame,
it spreads slowly, warms every cell so that like Whitman
I could sing myself, my eyes, waist, hips, every pore of rock.

I could sing every jazzy street in New York City.
Except I am afraid of the gloom, the dark again
after the sizzle of the national grid, night screams,
the dip of car lights in Chile. I want to retreat into silence
where a fox passes quiet as the red shadow of a cloud.
Our secret house inside the dynamo was safe.

* In 1943, the writer Edna St Vincent Millay began keeping meticulous records of the
dosage needed to feed her addiction, particularly to morphine and alcohol. Though
married to Eugene Boissevian until his death, she was for many years in love with the
poet George Dillon, for whom she wrote a sequence of sonnets.

I want to change the tense. When you move, death will visit
the new house in hippie clothes, in sharkskin elegance,
in purple lipstick and kohled eyes, coked up and snapping.
It's all the one to her. What's it to me if she makes you feel
ridiculous. The dark man is back. He has waited, faithful
as a lover. No jealousy. After all, we know the ending.

But it is necessary to say this – I received you like a sacrament
and though you expect too much of the vocative,
we found some joy. Such states are thresholds.
I weigh your voice against this script, ravens lift off the card,
wheel, circle. I spin the knife, put it away.
So much depends on timing, on how long grace lasts.

The King of the Cats

The King of the Cats is dead.
Odd how the knives and hollow-hearted stones
have known for weeks. Have seen it coming.
When the news is announced, spreads
from house to house, Kittys and Toms all over the kingdom
bounded out of windows frightening their people.
Each creature resorts to human speech.
They say, 'I have to go. The King is dead,'
and will not be disuaded. The females, all, it seems
old lovers, are the worst. They abandon families
where they are needed to go and mourn him.
Who was he? Small, puckish for a cat,
with his nine ex-wives used up – scarred
his drugged-fuelled escapades were as famous as his grin.
One stayed at home. She used her human voice to tell

how he alone among the cats possessed eloquence
and a mind of great beauty, tensile, with the span
and sureness of those high leaps he was admired for,
and a poet's vision but not a poet's voice, how once
he gave her the gift of his telescopic sight. It happened
as they walked in silence through a field at night
seeing all the mice rustling in the grass.
He pointed and she looked up, saw a star so close
she thought it would burn her with its cold light.
She asked him to take the gift back. He wouldn't.
It delighted him to leave his mark. She knew he was dead
when her sight turned normal. 'Good enough for him.
Now I can be domestic,' she said and slept.

Finis

Suddenly you're over like a book
or play, your little year, your starring role
in my life passed on to someone else.
Yes, a book I'll take from the shelf
in years to come and leaf through and find
the sprig of meadowsweet you handed
me that late June day still scents the pages
faintly; its frothy lace will have yellowed.

I won't remember the heron, you stopping the car,
the quiet walk to the river.
I'll recall your face vaguely, with distaste
or fondness, and that the sky was lavender
but nothing will give in my chest like the soft creak
when the spine, bent back too far, breaks.

The Wineapple

Daughter you are moving out and it is time
for this story about Demeter and Persephone.
You'll remember most of it from when
you were small: the working mother,
a strange lustre on the leaves the child gathers,
the ground opening, the man.
He shaded his eyes from the light, not the deed –
nowadays there is nothing that cannot be told.

You are moving out into the half-way house
and this is the story of half a year, childhood robbed.
It is the mother's point of view,
and we may differ on details as night from day
as daughters and their mothers do,
except in this: flower was your first full word.
You snatched one from the maelstrom of bougainvillea
at our neighbour's gate, an offering in magenta.

Some things are fated or let us say so with hindsight
because otherwise madness lies crouched in every night.
It is never as simple as it seems, this point of view.
There are daughters emerging from the ground
and mothers entering. But back to the story, the sound
of war between a woman and the king of hell. Demeter knew
from her own begetting that the gods' weaponry was crude
and would pay any ransom. A sullen bargain was made.

The gods fight dirty. So do mothers – they claw
time back line by line. The legend is told well. It sketches
over the uglier close ups. The story is hard enough
but not uncommon. He offered marriage and girls are tough.
So Zeus said. We know the cut earth bleeds as heavily now as when
the poem was written down and before that again
when the girl paused too long – it is said she ignored warnings –
by a stream and the new fruit died on the stem.

Remember the seeds in her teeth, how she had to stay
six months of every year with her kidnapper – you won't.
But on this cusp look carefully at the two houses of your life.
Choose neither. Wine. Apple. There's enough mapped out.
Separate juice from pulp. Rent a temporary room in the sun
and try to figure out what keeps so many stars from falling.
No, hardly hope. Will it add anything to say this is neither lament
nor epithalamium? All I can give you in spite of invocation

and the calling back of hard words piercing the silence
like sub-atomic particles is a splash of holy water, good perfume.
Touching, the invisible worlds physicists believe in despite new facts
that turn their temples inside out. This is the oldest story of all.
Open-ended. Home, the point of departure and return.
Among the jumble of skirts and jumpers waiting to be packed,
the gold shoes we chose together, for the heels and thongs
are impatient to be off. These are the bookends of your song.

Bowbend

Pink rain, a flock of waders turn in the sun
and there is nothing but the space between
dimensions, a luminous choreography
of the birds absence; a trick that
no matter how often we see it calls back
the ghosts of faith or wonder, to disappear again
perfectly rehearsed, like a shoal of mackerel
making their iridescent bellies dark.

Songs from the Beehive

For the sake of delight
Take from my hands some sun and some honey
As Persephone's bees enjoined on us.
                                    Osip Mandelstam

Autumn

I am not yet girl
not boy. Don't dare tell me
the kingdom of two rooms
coat covers, the river
flowing beyond the half-door
are nothing. Imprisoned fire.

Stitch this into history –
the hair on the dog
drowned under ice is the colour
of an old fox, of uaigneas,
the Irish for loneliness.

I am young still,
my belly a hole
howling to be filled. Firstborn
sole heiress to a fire in the grate,
desperate for its heat.

The hen's onyx eye pierces.
I will learn to fast her
for the kill – not fit
for the knife across her windpipe
nor to blow a shrill tune on it.

Daddy but for you
it would all be ash north of heaven.
The blue line after midnight
would flash once and grow dark.
I heard your voice last night
in a room in West Virginia.

Sisters gyre and whirl.
I try to step in on their beat
always a half-measure out.
They sweep out of reach
on the waves of a collapsing spectrum.

The women of the tribe
do not fuss. They form a sealed unit.
Think how wonderful to be right
about the map of heaven
the road home.
At least sometimes.

I am old now. I can see
the sun spinning into a burning string,
my fixed point going, going, gone.
The icy spikes' glow
on the holly tree
is the last brightness at the future's end.

Beyond could be anything or nothing.
It is not likely
to be the honeyplain.
While we have breath to sing,
let us or when the pain hits, scream.

Winter

Black hole, white dwarves
negative energy.
We'll arrange it all
into a neat ball of string
the end bits hidden
and unravel a skein of spectral light.

A thin girl
staring into black water
in 1975. A boy in a velvet jacket
wants to save her.
This black tide is no threat.
She steps towards it
in love with death.

Go back to her.
Let her stay as long as it takes.
No shape-shifters, no seal people
swim there – it is a sea of ink
out of which her hands will make
nothing or everything.

She knows the name
of this river and has drunk enough
to put all the ghosts under.
For years it worked.
You loved her, became the sun.
Suns expand, explode and go cold.

Walk the dry syke
the tearpath, its salt crystals
lit from within by some planetary light.
Not love, though something
holds the universe together still.

I am the girl
in the music box going round
and around in my tinkling world.
Let me wind down
or my head will explode
like a tired star. Give me your hand.

In Chicago, when you stood
by your father's grave
the wind knifed
the planes of your face raw.
A space opened around you,
frozen sound.

Wordprints. Crystal
imprints absail down the cliff
of your silence. I peered over the edge
and screamed from vertigo
and rage, beating the walls
of your chest for an echo.

This is the woman you married.
She has stood too long
looking at the Pleiades' light –
years after it has gone.
Do you know there are days when your skin
is part of mine still.

How can we count?
Twenty-two anniversaries.
Stop where? Your name is scripted
on every cell in black ink,
little rice-grains
some with Chinese characters.

The world needs re-making.
I am hopeless as a blind child.
There are unexpected ledges.
My son's arm around my shoulder
tells me where the edge is
and I step back.

Our eyes are stars,
houses. We fear eviction.
On all souls' night
a ghost horse drifts over the lake.
We wheel – we always will – between
the high and low solstices.

from *A Consideration of Silk* (1990)

Credo

There is a risk
that every consideration of silk,
each velvet hush between lovers
is stolen from other women.

That consenting acts of love
are only enjoyed
over the staked thighs
of the unsaved women of El Salvador,

that I have no right
to claim kinship with war women,
their ripe bellies slit like melons
while I guard

the contentment of my children,
agonise over which small
or great talent to nurture,
which to let die.

But while I am yet free
to observe the rights of womanhood
I will relish and preserve
the sigh, the sway, the night caress

yes, and the dignity of my children.
I will anoint my wrists with scent,
fold fine sheets, hoard
sheer stockings and grow a red rose.

I will hold them all for you
in an inviolate place,
the hallowed nook beside my heart
that no man knows.

Every step I dance
each glance of love and glistening note
from a golden saxophone
is an act of faith for I believe

in the resurrection of the damned.
I believe your day
is an arrow loosed,
it is burning along a silver bow

to meet you rising to your power
like a crocus in the snow.

Veronica

There is a place in Chile
where men from Europe go
to stare at the most distant stars
high in the mountains of the night.

Veronica was tortured for nine days
by ordinary men, for nine years,
for an infinite universe of time,
by ordinary men, with wives and kin.

Her heart stopped three times
but they did not let her die.
A doctor came to her aid
in a crackling white coat.
He prescribed precise doses of pain
and measured them with clean hands.
Still true to his Protean oath
he checked the pressure of her blood.

Veronica became the bricks
in her prison wall, impenetrable
when they raped her,

she became the fist
that smashed into her face
and when all they could do was done
she became the ragged scream.

She took the mantle
of unspeakable acts
when she set her mind to live
and raise her child.

Years later she found
there were things no mother could become:
the fire that consumed her son,
his crazed heartbeat,
the ditch they dumped him in,
so she became the hands
that soothed his dying feet.

Veronica cannot turn the page
while the rage of great crimes
burns over shallow graves.

There is a place in Chile
where no one dares to look
for vanishing stars,
a black hole in the hearts
of ordinary men.

Brushstrokes in Stone

Dona Amalia was made homeless
by South Africa in a casual kind of way.
The man in the government office said
where are your records to show
you were born in Namibia and if you were
what were you doing in Angola
on the twenty-fifth of April,
nineteen seventy four?

Sir, I am here. I, Amalia,

a woman of Africa. Give me my passport
to go home. There was a war.
My husband and my house are gone,
they have taken it all. Give me back my name.

Do you think I was never born?
That this hand, this small head,
this belly that has borne three children
is something I am making up to waste time?

You are holding me in paper chains.
My nights are filled with signatures
twisting like eels in a sea of blue forms,
they say they are important names.

Will no one believe the marks I have made?
This finger calloused from the needle,
these palms bleached like a fish's underbelly
from scrubbing marble floors.
I have left my brushstrokes in the stone
and my caress glows on my children's cheeks.

If I die waiting will you not give me
a little slip, signed and sealed to say
Amalia lived? A passport to eternity.
So why not give it to me now
and let me leave this place,
this powder blue nightmare
of stamps and notaries,
each stamp a brand of pain.

The official glanced up from his page,
Signora, he said, this petition is out of date.

Casa Pia

High among the pink peaks
    of the fading city
The vast house of my fears
    broods behind high gates –
The house of pity.

When I pass its closed face
    I taste ashes. A small boy
Haunts me with silence –
    the child of my heart calling
From the house of hidden joy.

The Journey

I

In the perpetual night
since you burned the retinae
out of my eyes with the white light
of your going, the question,
was it all lost,
the love, the labour, the blinding cost
has taken possession of my dreams.

Now the counting has started,
the moneymen reckon it all
in their primitive tally of wealth –
this much for good deeds,
less that much for death.
The question no one can silence,
was a life wasted?
Swishes at midnight around my room.

A black bat passes blind
across the silver moon,
the cruel comfortless moon.
It settles on my shoulder
like a cyst,

Oh callous moon, watcher of my descent
to the inner reaches, past
the last memory of rainbow rings,
to exile in a featureless place –
the soul.

Out there, no cosmic breath
Warmed me. No stentorian voice
chided me. No God called me.

In here, no cleansing tide
to rock me. No mountain nirvana,
no father to mind me.

Not even the sweet strain
of loss to cry for and make me melt
or drown me. No merciful death.

II

Now I am threshing the silence
in this birthplace of dreams,
whimpering. I have not yet learned
the nature of my crime,
but I know a mote's size.

Oh Maker, God! Show me the source,
an undeniable force of life
and I will even learn to float –
no more leaping like a salmon
against the world's tide.

This place is colder than atomic winter
and my voice is a frozen wave.

In the wastes of nothingness
no wind stirred for the night cries
to take wing.
All I saw with my burnt eyes
were grey cliffs and greyer mountains
and there was no turning away.
Who is to know the true shape
of the breeze lifting a leaf?
Deep and red and glistening with morning
a rose floated on an ocean of space.
Vision or mirage, it was enough

    To let in the dawn,
    just below the skin
    warmth spread in a velvet tide.

    I do not care to ask
    whether I sank or was buoyed up.

    Marina, what would you tell me
    about things that shine and dim?
    Your letters seem to give the lie
    to time, and you said yourself
    there must be no crying.

III

Often as I listen to living music
knowledge flows
across a sway of notes;
a not unfriendly shadow
acquired along the way,

I hardly mind it any more.
It bestows a certain peace,
like your absence,
merged now into tableaux vivants memories.
They grace the varied mansions
of your giving –
One quickens as all else fades –
at every unapproved crossroads
you were the first man dancing.

from *Where The Rocks Float* (1993)

Moyne Park

i.m. George Macbeth

Cad a dheanfaimid feasta gan adhmad?
Ta deireadh na gcoillte ar lar;

                                    Cill Cais

The heart is still in the great house.
You graced it with an interval of decency.
Fine-plumed to the end like the doomed swan
beating its way through a blinding storm
to crash against the quivering glass
you sat, beating out your last breath
in sonnets, silent in a golden morning room,
avoiding nothing; your marriage of manners and rage.

But the life, George! We who were dispossessed
made free in borrowed elegance, made an entrance
and silently I exulted. From those high cold rooms
any of us could have ridden forth, sleek with assurance.
When you left, the house died. I will not mourn it.
Thanks to you, I would no longer burn it.

Canvas Currach

I am a racer. Light, made for speed.
I hardly touch the water. Fragile
but I can carry three big men
and outlast them. It's all in the balance.
I will never drown.

I have no sail to wear but my black dress
clings to my ribs, seamless.
I am a slim greyhound of the sea.
The deeper your oars dig in
the lighter I skim.
I am built to run. Race me!

The Maighdean Mhara

It is always the same,
the men say little and the women talk,
guessing what the men are saying
in the long gaps between words.
Always fishing for clues
they drop barbs, make humorous casts
in an endless monologue of lures.
They'll say anything for a bite.
The men look hunted and stay silent.

But I can make them sing out
a shower of curses and commands.
I challenge them to win
against the sea and other men.
They listen for the slightest whisper
between me and the wind. They understand
my lightest sigh, and respond.

Here in my belly where men feel safe
I draw out their soft talk,
rising, falling, low as breath.
At ease and sure of their control
they are, in Irish, eloquent.
I never let on anything
but fall and rise and humour them.

Grainne's Answer to Burke's Proposal*

Take me for one year certain
hot and cold and strong.
What woman will give you
as much for that long?
A year in a wild place.
Take me or leave me as I am.

* Burke's proposal was marriage '… for one year certain'. This was permissible under
Brehon Law.

Cealtrach*

The children were never told
about those places. The unbreachable
silence of women protected us
from terrible things.
We heard the dread whisperings
and peopled the swarming spaces with ghosts.

Yet we never knew. They buried
unnamed innocents by the sea's edge
and in the unchurched graveyards
that straddled boundary walls. Those infants
half-human, half-soul were left
to make their own way on the night shore.

Forbidden funerals, where did mothers
do their crying in the two-roomed cottages
so beloved of those Irish times?
Never in front of the living children.
Where then? In the haggard, the cowshed,
the shadowed alcoves of their church?

That Christian religion was hard.
It mortified the flesh
and left mothers lying empty,
their full breasts aching, forever afraid
of what the winter storms might yield,
their own dreams turning on them like dogs.

* One of the names for a burial ground for unbaptised children, usually spanning the
boundary between two fields and often close to the seashore.

The Visit (i)

The little girl tightened
the belt on her skimpy
homemade cotton dress,
knowing her clothes marked her,
that even her polished shoes were wrong.
But she smiled as she burned,
shame corseted her frame,
buckled the words
coming out of her mouth,
making even her accent a misshapen thing.

She longed and she hated
but she spoke
every time one of them came
graciously, to visit her mother.

Ave (iv)

The little girl played
in her overturned boat,
her church, her shop, her sailing ship.
The only architecture she knew
had the vaulted roof
of a sawn in two pucán.
She plainchanted with the cuckoo
and *Ave, Ave, Ave Maria*
was the song she learned at school.

When they asked how many children
she could see the pained looks
overcome the breeding.
She felt like scabies or the mange,
infectious and poor.

The Shape of Saying (ix)

They call it Received English
as if it was a gift you got
by dint of primogeniture.
Maybe it was. Old gold words
toned like concert violins,
tuned to talk to God.

After the French and Latin wars
I relished the poppies of Donne
though I thought this graceful foreign tongue
was only meant for men –
all right for the likes of Coleridge
but it gave me unpleasant dreams.

They say we cannot speak it
and they are right.

It was hard and slippery as pebbles,
full of cornered consonants
and pinched vowels, all said
from the front of the mouth –
no softness, no sorrow,
no sweet lullabies –
until we took it by the neck and shook it.

We sheared it, carded it, fleeced it
and finally wove it
into something of our own,
fit for curses and blessings
for sweet talk and spite,
and the sound of hearts rending,
the sound of hearts tearing.

Ghost (xi)

There is little mention here
of grandmothers and mothers
for this is the book
of fishermen and Englishmen.
They hounded me and minded me,
they shone like gods for me
and burned all others out of the sky.

One man at home among visions,
one not given to ghosts;
one that wrote of bravery and drowning,
one that lived it.

What could she do to match them?
She heard only the cries
out of the night depths,
the sighs of the unclaimed drowned
haunted her bedroom at the gable end.

She was sure that some awful sight,
a soaked soul,
would break the night waters
below Doon Hill and come to her
shivering in the moonlight
to plead for burial.

After a frozen moment
she would shimmer and dissolve
like stained glass in a fire,
leaving a blot
like an unconfessable sin,
a black spot on the tongue.

from *The Knife in the Wave* (1997)

Miss Panacea Regrets

i

Give in! Don't you know no one escapes
the power of creatures reaching out with breath alone?
                                        Marina Tsvetayeva

I have lost May but it surfaces here.
Each time a breath lifts it from the page
it rises, a moon gleaming like an old sixpence.

They have pierced my breast.
The wound, unstitched, blossomed
and like Philoctotes I am unhealed.
All that lovely month I limped on half-sail,
half-life in the rose scented mornings,
A hot-house virgin on a May altar.

Yes, there are shafts of pain
Dark and no one knows their depth.
Is there no one to burn for me like a black candle?
Who dares to pray?
Marina, I would hold your pain
but who would contain mine?
It rages through the dawn
blazing the lyric down
and blackening all the hawthorn.

My pain is hungry and lean.
It licks the skin, eats shame slowly
and wolfs through to the bone
but the real work, the slow burn
is in the sinews, like a poem.
That's what the man said – a bit slight
but sinewy all the same. Not tough enough, I felt.
The wolf is tearing at my chest.

Men with knives surround me.
It is half past one.
They will come at two
for the third time to cut into my chest
and release a thousand roses.
The instructions – between the fourth
and fifth ribs – are precise.
It is all done without screaming,
without making a fuss.
I am not brave. 'I can't.'
It is my own thin voice.
I have no shame, no control.

You will not stitch breath
with such blunt instruments.
Use salve, some ungent made with herbs.
Pray to Hygeia, Apollo, Panacea
For a drug to help us tolerate
the mercury heavy air.

A youth in a white coat walks away.
He has stitched in the uncoiling thorns.
He is a climber bagging peaks.
Pain is not his business –
not quantifiable like the carcass.
Is that Shylock peeking around the screen
and Polonius behind the arras?
The colour of St Teresa's ward is hideous.
My husband comforts me.
A nurse holds me down.

I have been betrayed and time
is an altered state. It coils and flattens
like a sea snake.
The days of the dead
follow. I know I am dead and there is nowhere
else to go, for ever and ever amen.
I am crying all night for my children.

Is there no one to lay a head
against my torn breast and listen
to my ragged breathing?

What you hear with your stethoscope
is not the true beat of her heart
merely a counterpoint
to the rush and whisper of blood.

Not knowing this you say
'This woman is afraid.
She craves sympathy.'
With palms upturned when she has failed
you tell her looking unconvinced
'We are not God.'
She knows but sometimes
you are all there is.

They have pierced my breast.
The double edge of doctor's hands
squeeze from me the stangled inhalation
of birth. When the pain subsides
there is a shudder, a child's endless desolation.
It is dangerous to let
all the grieving women
loose like this. They could drown you
in their funeral sighs.

I am small and broken on an iron bed
anchored in the Regional Hospital
where they mostly do what they can
but brook no talk of pain. Its implements
are too blunt, the sledgehammer,
the jagged glass,
the drops of molten lead. It is all rack
and ruin here after midnight.
An island woman moans.
This, she says, is not my real face.
Lady Morphia sneers and walks away
with her white coat open
and her black hair loose.

I flounder in a storm of wasted breath:
The times I didn't dance a requiem waltz
for the forgotten dead,
my chastised children's tears,
the forbidden noun of a name
launched into the waiting night
is lost in the wake
of the poem not spoken, the prayer not said.
I could end this voyage
with my keel on top yet.

They have pierced my flesh.
The wolf is snarling at my bed.
He never leaves me – when I sleep
His low growl tatters the edge of my dreams.
I tell my children it's a dog
that only barks because he is afraid.
Soon he will go away.
They are unconvinced
by this American psychology.

I am tired. A friend will emerge
to ring the hospital with silver bells.
(And garlic, she quips, for Doctor Death.)
There will be red and purple roses
raging at dawn and in the end there will be time
to say the long Magnificat
or not. Mind me. I am tired.
All that ancient grief chokes me.
There is lead in my veins.
Let me sleep. I am tired
keeping planes up,
high buildings from falling on my children
fending the dragons that enter my room,
feeding the dragons that hold up the moon.

Look, someone has brought delphiniums.
Their blue closes over me, cool as peace.

O open this day with the conch's moan, Omeros
as you did in my boyhood, when I was a noun
gently exhaled from the palate of the sunrise.
                                              Derek Walcott

Lady Morphia enters.
This time she is a woman my own age.
'I will control your pain' she says.
'This, after all, is nineteen ninety two',
and busies herself with needles
the way certain women do. I cry
short jerky tears. A hand on my shoulder
welcomes me to Mercy Street.
My words of thanks tear like asbestos.

They have bruised my flesh.
A black Homer is salving
incurable wounds in the No Pain Cafe,
He has fashioned me a line
of perfect weightlessness to say.
I grasp the golden thread
and enter the labyrinth afraid.

.... A long pause.
One. Two. Three. Four
carries on, a metronome.
I enter gasping on the last beat
afraid as ever that a line
is measured by the breath.
The wolf is licking at my throat.

First the swelling bubble ooh.
I watch the sound grow
A valley of echoes
the sweet call of an island Homer,
the unheard birth cry of my daughter.
The poet's silver sheaves of light
are stooked above me in the dark.

I breathe.
In, out. In, out. I float
on the precise lightness of vowels.
Each one I exhale is faintly haloed
like a Czechoslovakian Christ.
The wolf is nuzzling at my throat.

It has been excised,
a weak spot in my breath
cut out and the tear stitched.
It is healing well. In time
it will become a faint mark,
my stolen language, an echo that tugs,
the need for a word not known
like grá or brón for love or pain.
Neither direct nor wrong.

They have changed my resonance,
stretched me tight as a drum.
Every ripple in the air plays me.
It is time to undertake
the rehabilitation of my voice,
the only instrument I play.
All that fire and ripped air
have cracked it.

It is retuned slowly,
the throat stretched,
the column of breath urged to my needs –
I have no patience
and worst of all no guarantee.
My own body
is making strange
like someone else's baby.

Poems like spears
pin me between earth and sky.
The moon sneers. In daylight
the sharp planes of colours
mean nothing will ever be as good
again and mean no more.
The coral sand in my fingers
grain on separate grain

is as undependable as the sun.
I know nothing of what this means
and all that can be said
is that no other world
would make Whitman roar
his grassy prayer
and the air holds power to cut or love me.

I have seen words made flesh,
whether poetry or delirium,
sanctuary lamps
that burned when the sun
quenched. Well, this is where it started,
the dark, every cell clenched, breath.
This time, diphthong before consonant.

The Wound

Nothing changes. The legend tells of three men
in a currach, fishing.
A big sea rose up and threatened to engulf them.

They cast lots to see who was wanted – a young man.
As the swell hung over him
he grabbed a knife and pitched in desperation,

cold steel against the wave.
The sea withdrew and all were saved.
One man heard a cry of pain and prayed.

At nightfall a woman on a white horse
enquired and found the house.
'My mistress is sick and only you can save her,'

she said and gave him guarantees.
They took the road under the sea
to a palace where a beautiful woman lay.

His knife was buried in her right breast.
'This is the knife you cast into my flesh.
You must pull it out with a single stroke,

or I will die by midnight.' He did
and the wound became a rose. She offered
the treasures of her green underworld,

a pagan kiss. The same old story. She begged:
'This scar will ache forever if you go.'
Then a choir of lost men whispered,

'Stay here and she will have your soul,'
so he blessed himself, refused and went above
to the simple solid world he understood.

A Touch of Sass

Once I saw a black woman with sass
conducting English like a big band,
words danced and a jazz chant
two-stepped across the floor.
Sounds rocked and rolled, vowels
stretched and yawned and sighed
as Maya Angelou put some revolution
in the elocution class.
I closed my eyes and smiled
and thought of England.

Interior

'There is no domestic detail in her poems ...'

There is now. Two by fours
and concrete slabs, the floors
littered with cigarette stubs.

The timber supporting the new stairs
is stalwart. 'That won't shift.'
It will of course and it's all useless

when the electrician's mate
kangoes through the live wire
playing a mean guitar.

Good Golly, Miss Molly. 'Draw a straight line
up from the switch, in your mind.
That's called an image,' I told him,

but they're only interested in grouting
and gully risers, a consonance of solid things,
nuts and bolts men.

The skin of ochre paint in the bedroom
has done more to hold this house together
than a gross of six inch nails.

'There's a fault in the living-room walls.
It could be the wrong shade of red – Atomic Flash.'
Like Gods, they never listen.

Geis*

I marked him young
and waited while he tended his book learning.
I watched him dig and grow strong,
soon he could plane and polish a song.
He breathed deep and learned rhythm
rowing currachs in the Carna sun.

He was a singer and the son of singers.
I let him play and led him to the well.
When his wild days were over
I saw him drink with a bog thirst.
A thousand songs! Oh, he was fine
my young king of the sky.

London, Newport, Philadelphia, New York:
the path was laid out. All he had to do was sing.
His face became the perfect mask
for spirits older than a priest's blessing
to speak through and when he sang.
No other woman had a chance.

In return I put the burn of a turf fire,
the swish of a girl's bright skirt,
the ring of a horseshoe on stone in his voice.
In return, I was the woman with red hair
watching his black eyes quench
when the last note snagged in his throat.

* An Enchantment, a spell.

Note: Both Geis and Caoineadh Mháire are part of a suite of poems broadcast on RTE as part of a documentary on Joe Heaney, the Conamara sean-nos singer.

Caoineadh Mháire*

Why do we love men that are bad for us –
are we that weak? Hardly the kisses,
fruit in the mouth soon melts.
His Spaniard's eyes never settled on me right
but the mouth music lured me.

There was something old about his voice
that took the city ground from under me
and brought little yellow shells
scattering up the back streets of Glasgow.
Oh he was handsome, though, like a stag.

When I felt the fine sand
between my toes I should have run
to the nearest forgettable city boy
and chanced the ordinary,
but he sang and I was caught.

I listened as the hook eased in,
listened for the blas he put on my name
until all I could hear was my own breath
like the tide in a cave, echoing, going out
and the children crying.

A grey crow settled on my chest
and took his time.
A high price for a slow song:
'A Pheadair, a Aspail, an bhfaca tu mo ghra bhan?
Ochon agus ochon o.'**

* Máire's Lament
** 'Peter, Bishop, Have you seen my sweet boy?'
   The poem refers to one of the best-known religious laments. It is sung by Mary
   for Christ. It is intimate and powerful and possibly part of a tradition influenced
   by medieval French singing.

Knell

I want to write a simple poem
with the taste of green apple,
clear as a high bell. A poem
seamless as a grey chemise that fits
like water, and not make a fuss for once

but ordinary men are raping children
no older than my daughter.
They are invading their small bodies
like missiles while Europe stares.
Every mother knows the way to stop them.

An old man is burning sticks
in the basement of the Europa hotel.
In the playing fields of Sarajevo
goosesteps echo. A toddler,
his belly embroidered with schrapnel, screams.

I fear the cold silence of Europe.
It colours the apple's aftertaste,
slows down the tune, prints seams of blood
on the silk. And all over Ireland
the bells are coming down.

The Lightcatchers

For Maeve on her eleventh birthday

St Brigid's Day comes storming in,
I make my act of faith in Spring.
The mystery of planting – what grows
in bleak or lush places is on us.
A courgette swells from orange flowers
and the untilled rock yields sea thrift.

We reaped the wind and you came
child of hibiscus and cinnamon.
No statue from a cold museum
you spark and shine through every room
in the house. Home is the husk.
Soon you will shuck it off to go dancing.

Look how for centuries we nourished sons,
buried the girl children, bound their feet.
Did we think it would make no difference?
As we slouch towards the millennium
the portents are all for the world ending.
Soldiers are sprouting along every border.
They are tumbling
out of their mothers' wombs with guns.

Something has changed.
You are eleven this St Brigid's Day.
Last year's party girls in coloured dresses
are swirling over our honey timbered floor,
a carousel of lightcatchers
tinkling like Christmas chimes.
This year they will be more faceted still.
The music slows.

I hang a cross of fresh rushes.
There is a stretching under the ground,
a reaching for the sun.
Brid, open your throat and bless them!
Let this treasury of minded daughters
planted as sapphires
ripen across the continents into rubies.

Meditation on the Long Walk

Desire would be a simple thing
all those Gods rampant
and the earth moving for Leda;
her life transformed by his seed,
what was engendered revealed,
the mystery of what she understood
economically preserved
in a ripple of uncluttered hindsight.

Flip the coin and let the wives out.
Yeats' telling questions hang
upside down like fish-hooks
or inverted swans' necks. With her beak
savage at his loins
indifferent to all but his seed
is there talk of ecstacy and knowledge
among the tumbling feathers?

Yet there is an attractive symmetry,
that lust without responsibility
she peeled back to pure desire
him a real God, the earth
pulsing briefly like a star
and a few thousand years away
a poet trawling the night sky
for a single blinding metaphor.

The Otter Woman

Against the wisdom of shore women
she stood on the forbidden line too long
and crossed the confluence of sea and river.
One shake of her body on O'Brien's bridge
and the sea was off her.
A glorious swing from haunch to shoulder
sent water arching in the sunlight,
a fan of small diamonds flicked open,
held, fell. Her smooth pelt rose into fur.

He stood and watched her from the shadows
and moved to steal her tears
scattered on the riverbank.
Now he could take his time. He smoked.

She was all warm animal following the river,
trying her new skin like a glove.
He trailed her, magnetised by her power to transform,
the occasional bliss on her face, her awakened body.
Once or twice she saw him.
Her instincts were trusting on land.
They smiled. This took the whole Summer.

He took her by a lake in Autumn
a sliced half moon and every star out
the plough ready to bite the earth.

She left him on a street corner
with no choice and no glance back,
Spring and a bomber's moon.
In between their loosed demons
played havoc in the town.

He pinned her to the ground, his element.
This was not what she came for
but what she got.
Soon the nap of her skin rose only for him.
It was too late to turn back.
She grew heavy out of water.

Indifferent to all but the old glory
he never asked why she always walked
by the shore, what she craved,
why she never cried when every wave
crescendoed like an orchestra of bones.

She stood again on the low bridge
the night of the full moon.
One sweet deep breath and she slipped in
where the river fills the sea.
She saw him clearly in the street light – his puzzlement.
Rid of him she let out
one low strange cry for her human sacrifice,
for the death of love
for the treacherous undertow of the tribe
and dived, less marvellous forever in her element.

Song of the Wise Woman

Speak to me of tapestry
Speak to me of gold
Speak to me
Of a flowering tree
Watered by a woman's blood.

Read to me of hanging stars
Read to me of love
Read me that dark talking tree
That hides a secret child.

Sing away the dark man's touch
For I am still and cold
Sing me air and sing me fire
With your voice of Wintery gold.

Whisper me a legend
Whisper me a lie
Whisper me a flowering tree
And warm me in its fire.

Weave me in your tapestry
Thread me through with gold
But I must tend the Winter tree
Watered by a woman's blood.

The Annunciation

History is teeming with comely maidens
awaiting godly transformations.

Leda, Yourself and the Conneely* girl
must have felt the same fear

when used as host
by swan, merman and Holy Ghost.

This given, did He have to send
such a fey announcing angel round

with a mouth like a jaded sex tourist,
or is this where God bows to the artist?

All three know the transformation
from luscious girl to Pieta

pregnant, on the run, crucified with tears
will take three months less than thirty-four years,

that you will then bear nineteen centuries
of prayers for airports, intercession, cures.

Did a trace of that plundered innocence
tint the rose windows of Notre Dame with radiance?

Here, where people carried knives
between them and marauding spirits

* The Conneelys were said, in folklore, to be descended from seals.

when they sang your lament in triplicate**
in words familiar and intimate

the litany of limb and feature by destroyed mothers
stopped the hand of Gods and artists.

** The lament in triplicate is that referred to in 'Caoineadh Mháire'.

Forgive Me that I am Coping Badly

After Akhmatova

There is no use bringing politics into it,
I would have coped as badly in any gender
at times like this, with breath pinched
to show that it is rationed,
words rioting on all sides
and my cinnamon daughter
spreading honey on my final, final manuscript.
What has happened to my organised life
when disaster was 'Saturday night
and not a child in the house washed'?

from *Asylum Road* (2001)

On my first visit after the solstice,
delayed by a good storm,
the woman in the stone house spoke:
'I will rise and drink the morning
even this grey daylight
that is neither sunny nor beautiful
but stuck like a half-torn rag
on a holly bush, a plastic bag in a doorway
at the fag end of the century,' she greeted me.

'I will rise and eat the black clouds
that stick in my craw
because they are merciful and hide
the bloody necklaces of Kosovo,
the planes over Baghdad,
the cold faces of the subsidy-checkers in Dublin,
stemming what comes in on the tide;
not knowing that flotsam and jetsam
is what keeps coastal people going. But I tell you,
she said they have lives of pure misery,
such misery as you never saw –

halfpence and pence.'
She got up and took in gulps
of bad weather and dressed herself in tattered clouds,
magnificent in her own way. Then we breakfasted.
She poured tea into duckegg cups.
'I always liked fine china'
and the fire reddened in the grate
and we ate the bad morning and it did us no harm.
'We'd make great queens,' she remarked,
'Or a damned sight better than what's there.'
We looked out over the waves. 'A big sea.'
She made an elegant arc of her arm, trailing cumulii.

'That is an Area of Scientific Interest
according to Brussels.
Did you ever meet a bureaucrat?'
she asked as if I might have unwittingly entertained
one in my home,
his pointy hooves hidden in patent leather shoes
they being practiced in the art of surprise.
'Talking golf-sticks, most of them.
They wouldn't care if I was ten miles out past Slyne Head
clinging to a barrel so damn their souls to hell.'
We drank our Barry's tea.
Charity may be all very well for those
that lie on under the covers on cold mornings
but not for women in stone houses
at the edge of the sea.

The Loose Alexandrines

Shameless they parade twelve by twelve by twelve across
the pages out of uniform. They wear high heels,
one with dyed blonde hair has a run in her stockings
and another of very unresolved gender

though I predict he will have a feminine end
and it serves him right – is dancing over the line
dressed in leather pants with a big star on his crotch.
It lights up – now what do you think he got that for?

Not his prosody. Look what happens as soon as
you relax the rules. First they make up their own. Soon
they're stravaiging over the pages in loose ranks.
Total anarchy – where's the poetry in that?

Muck savages, socialists, up from the country,
I disapprove of the regions and those people
without so much as a degree from Trinity,
with relations in Boston instead of Blackpool

marching out with the best of us. The Atlantic!
The poetic equivalent of red lipstick.
Books must be prescribed – more Larkin, less Yeats, no Plath.
No mad women – you're safe with Bishop and Clampitt.

Poetry must be strict and purge itself to survive.
It's time to round them up and herd them, twelve by twelve
by twelve into sheep pens, the lads divided from
the girls, the pigs from the pearls, the boys from the men.

The Spanish Lady

What, you ask, made me want to get away?
Things that happened. Or didn't – you know how it is.
A dream of wrecked ships across the moon,
the belief, growing into certainty, that I was born
in Fuento Vaqueros in Southern Spain.
Years later, when an old man handed me
a red carnation in the Granada sun
I knew I had followed the right dream.

Have no fear I will forget the quotidian,
your beloved particular. Who could imagine
the effect of oranges on a child reared on rock;
what desire is squeezed into her thin hand
reaching for the home-from-hospital fruit,
the fire in those small dimpled suns?

The Ballad of Pepsi and Wonderbra

Mr Diet Coke met Miss Wonderbra
whose legs are in the Guinness Book of Records
– for length – on mid-morning radio.
'Hello, he said, so you're in Dublin
I'm in Dublin too. Let's meet,' and then
they swapped vital statistics on the air.
She started it. 'How tall are you?' she asked.
When he said her bosom would be in line with his…
'Hey guys, the line is live.'
The would-be shock jock tried to get back
into the conversation
he had started with salacious
talk of bosoms, thighs, the hard job
of finding a woman to equal Mr Coke or Pepsi's
charms. He who had only recently been saved
from being torn apart on that very same show
by secretaries driven mad with lust.
It seems he has the secretaries of Ireland
baying at the moon with desire which confirms
my suspicion of office work.

'She can't cook,' the presenter said, as if cooking
was a dirty word. She giggled and quickly passed
to talk of uplift. I thought there was a lot to be said
for certain Latin American books on the culinary arts,
even Calvino's thoughts on chilis, but decided
this was not the time to phone in. I also wondered
what legs had to do with it and wasn't she wasted on a bra
and did she double job for Pretty Polly?
Then there were his legs, which got no airing.
That's hardly gender equality, now is it?
'We'll talk to you nearer your destination,'
the presenter said to remind her she was on a job.
'Oh yeah,' she said, 'whatever,' and resumed
the real conversation until he cut them off.
I hate it when they do that.
Now we'll never know his height.

Anubis in Oghery

For Oisin

Our dog, Georgie is dead. She lived
with us for ten years and walked three miles a day
with me but loved you best because she was
mostly yours. Now I have to watch your face
the reddening look, as if it might break open
and think there is something about a man's pain
that cracks like chestnuts or old timber.
It is not lubricated by tears.

You buried her down among the hazels
and blackberries, made a cairn on the grave
planted two birch trees. No one instructed you
in these rites. Yesterday you were a small boy
playing with a pup that chewed windows. Now
you walk away, a dream dog at your heel. Tall, able.

The Abandoned Child

This is a simple photograph, a black and white picture
of a child lying in the dust. She has no name.
Call her Baby, Beauty, Unbeloved, she is the face of our time.

She is thrown on the earth afraid, abandoned at the limit
of word and note and brushstroke.
Every poem pauses here. Important questions are decided:

Who will feed the child, the price of corn, what happens
to the planets when they die; and how long
do the doomed beauties last with the cameras gone?

The theory holds that a shrunken star will collapse
into a ball so tight, not even light will escape.
Into this invisible hole anything may fall, and has.

As to the children, the books are silent or advise
metaphorical distance. Only the songs remember
the unbreachable chasm between jazz notes,

where dead loves hang. She would be twenty,
maybe twenty-five now, a wife, a washerwoman, a physicist
spreading chaos across the stars. In her alternative Universe

there would be dishes to be washed, children to be
sent to school and minded. She might even now
be writing up a formula on her IBM compatible,

a theorum to predict the trajectory of a mother's kiss
but in the known world money changed hands. Prisons filled
and the crowd stampeded. She is most likely dead.

She has no name, this beauty lying in the dirt
between well made sonnets and free verse,
without an I or you or us, between the hand's release

and the rattle of the Gorta box. Read her eyes.
The Universe is made up in equal measure of tears
and hunger and bits of string, the old dimensions

and her face has more agony than a medieval Christ.
Her poem is the soundless howl of light streaming
into the black hole of heaven. Trying eternally to get out.

The Pearl Sonnet

Now that the donor of it all was dead
she could have it fixed. In the confusion
after the funeral whether the rope frayed
or was tugged, it broke and all the pearls
were re-strung exactly in the right order – but one.
It had always taken the light differently,
irritated the others, not unlike the grain of sand
that was its own conception. Now it was gone.
The necklace glowed, its cool elegance displayed
on public occasions. The missing pearl
was not forgotten – its absence defined how well
the others matched. It was re-set as a pendant.

It hangs at someone else's throat now and looks
well enough, like a tear or an unshed moon.

The Joiner's Bench

Somehow she found herelf drawn
to his desk, that intimate place,
ran her hand over its surface
as you would smooth a skirt down.
A ridge where the lathe had skipped
delayed her and she looked up at his eyes
surprised how familiar
their blue black stain. It spread like ink.

His mind played over her poems,
her hand slipped over the scarred timber,
A wave of slim-fingered elegance. Best left at this.
Best to have set the ocean on fire
between them than a shared desk –
trees were her nemesis.

Violation

Blue grass can still be bought and so can 'Le Must
du Cartier' in case you thought to ask
later in a different poem and 'Je Reviens'
can still be sung.

This country of ours is violent,
I think to myself this morning with surprise –
I only lately realised that dancehall fights
were not as usual everywhere, nor everywhere excused
as young men going wild. I mean in Connemara, not Belfast.
Half-murdering your neighbour at a dance
at Christmas and St Patrick's Day
was not, it seems, considered de rigeur
for young men everywhere but there it is:

Women of good breeding in the West
retired after a good look from balcony or chair
to the toilets to repair the damage caused by sweat, fear
and excitement, as etiquette demanded.

I never understood the impulse to pulverise flesh
with bricks or bats but – let's stick
to what we know – an arc just like a reaping hook and deep
opens across a dancer's cheek, stops just below the eye,
follows a neighbour's practiced crack, the whiskey bottle
smashed across a bench, and – 'Say that again, you bastard.'
This tableau surprised but did not shock.
Later I found the jagged weapon on the floor
marked 'Paddy' like an English joke.

Those men had wives at home, and daughters,
were kind to me, respectful always.
We were schooled in such accommodations
as women made with men's natures. Why is it then
I see the drops of blood like garnet beads
before a watery liquid joined the dots,
my neighbour's eyes, feral, nothing familiar there but lust;
why when history's black hags dive into our personal sky
at inappropriate times, the woods are full of hump-backed beasts
and all the lovely dancing girls emerge
from Kosovo and Africa and places around here
with their giggling dreams in rags around their breasts?

Wanted, Muse

Are you young, female with long legs?
Mysterious eyes, any colour
but the blacker the better,
Rosaleen. Degree optional though it is

essential to be literate – you'll be required
to read the poet's work, to distinguish
his gifts from his attributes – analysis
won't be necessary. A nice smile, for 'she smiled'

and a tendency to appear shrouded in mist
early in the morning, but only when
accompanying the poet on his visits
to the country – aishlingi* are passé in the town.

Blonde is good, dark preferred.
Love of cheap wine and travel combined
with a talent for exciting writing lust
is vital. As for the hair, dye if you must.

Are you young, male, with long legs and bi-
lingual skills? Poetry is an equal opportunity employer.
Gardening and good biceps are a priority.
Sigh if you must, but remember, poets value muscularity.

* An Aishling is a vision poem.

Macchu Picchu, Inis Mór*

For Pura Lopez Colome

On the ferry out we talk about marvels:
the poet that left a mistress for his wife –
and translate images; they break the surface
of our talk like new islands. To the west
a red heart bleeds over the airstrip,
to the east, licked by terracotta flames
a Daz-white angel is fighting the devil for a soul –
he pulls desperately on one leg
but the devil has him by the head. The soul
scorched and nearly torn in two
is wearing a bainín** jacket and Reebok trainers –

it must be the Gaeltacht they're intent on saving.
He is hacking at them both
with a rusty halo bent into a T na G logo.***
What would that mean in Mexico?
Well, you tell me in accented English,
'The little guy in the middle is the loser.'
The devil spins around and flashes us a smile
like Al Pacino. I chant O'Flatharta's ode to the cregg,
which flowers as we roam the island.
Small fields of primroses and gentians
have the terrible freshness of lost children.

Here sweet accidents are married to hard labour.
Poets make uneasy pagans.
Chiapas, you say, Chiapas, and tell me
that in Mexico there would be red earth.
'And scorpions' to give the last line bite.
We have sirens and seashells in common
though later at Dun Aengus I angle
in case. This small stone citadel
my body out from the clefts in the limestone.
is no match for Oaxaca or Macchu Picchu
but it serves the same purpose –

---

*   The poem arises from a conversation between two poets about poetry on a day
    trip to Inis Mór.
** Traditional homespun woollen jacket.
*** The Irish Language Television Channel.

as good a place as any to start the past,
to offer gifts of older Gods,
Celtic or Mayan, it doesn't matter;
They are idols of our own desire to comfort
those who swept up the mess
left by torture, emigration, famine,
again and again and again. The ones that were left.
There must have been more to their lives than this,
we think, they must have had simple faith,
if only in the dead partying along the seashore,
the caoin**** of a guitar, white roses on the water.

Canvas Currach II

The black canvas drawn like a dress
over the ribs is skin this time.
Not even a treacherous shift
separates her from the waves.

The people on this coast know the sea
holds or gives up whom she will
and yields occasional miracles – coral,
gold coins, ambergris.

She shoulders up the lumps of water
between her and sanctuary
as good as the oarsmen she has drawn;
they are her luck, and the red-tipped oars

dip like fingers into a sea of bones.
She makes shore. Now all depends
on what they call this sleek stranger –
jetsam or treasure.

**** Keen.

These are not Sweet Girls*

*'After every war
Someone has to tidy up.'*
Wislawa Szymborska

The wounds women inflict softly on women
are worse than any lover can do
because they are more accurate. Such women
lead from behind in silence. They are Ophelia's big sisters,
the marrying kind, their power, mediated through men.
Their smiles hook around rivals' throats
like necklaces. They are sweet in company.

Then there are women who know about night,
those who have read the wind correctly and understand
the real business of the world
could be decided by women alone
and be better managed – but want men
for their honest lies, a door held open, a thorny rose:
they are always promising something.

I myself am happy to barter the well-run shop
for sweet rain, a hand steadying my shoulder
like a wave.
Only this morning a man's mercury shadow
ran through my fingers when I woke.
He drained through my sleep. For hours
I heard a voice in the upstairs rooms – echo, echo.

Such men are first principles – they represent themselves
poetry, lust. They lie with honesty that women lack
and take our breath away with masterpieces,
like Rodin's stolen kisses or the portraits
of Picasso's mistresses, one after another.
Somewhere between their eyes and the wine
we recognise need and admit the honest truth :

* *These Are Not Sweet Girls* 'Poetry by Latin American Women', White Wine
Press, New York.

These are the world's great lovers,
the men who like women.
Such a man will write one hundred love poems
to wife number three
and she will let herself be taken in. Such a man
causes sensible women to wear high heels,
skirts, hearts on our silk blouses like statues.

We pay attention briefly to our own desires
over the wants of our children
who orbit us like small moons – this is why we love them.
You Latin women are not fooled.
When he leaves you say: 'Such bastards.'
and 'Love has done this to me',
as if love happens to women,

governing them like a verb, or the moon.
You laugh at his photograph appearing
in a bookshop six thousand miles away
as if that was the least he could do, you both
being Catholic. Apparitions of lovers are commonplace
in South America. Here, it's saints.
You are not nice girls.

In the face of cancer and betrayal you open the whiskey
smoke cigars and kick off your shoes.
This is the real constituency of women
where it is not enough to sweep up the mess
when unspeakable things are done
to your children. You insist
there has to be singing, a dance in the face of death.

Committed

The woman in the bed
in the hospital for the mad
in Ballinasloe shrivelled
under a thin blanket.
'May the curse of Almighty God
burn the ground from under
that lightening bitch' –
the nurse that reported
'No improvement' to the doctor.
Then her voice collapsed
in on itself like a tent.
'Ask them to get me out,' she said.
'Tell them to bring me home' –
her eight grown children.

The visitor was young and frail
in that department herself.
She spent the next ten years afraid
of the guard, a parent,
a doctor with a pen gathered
to commit her. The sin was fear
of the dark, the Blessed Mother's eyes
following her, being left alone
with the replay of a ruined voice
winding down.
At the end of a decade
she packed her black
lace mantilla and went to Spain,
found a lover with soft eyes,
was able to ignore
the tortured Jesus statues
that celebrate death –
this was suffering worth
going to Heaven for.

Best of all, she made a home
in their language. The words
quickened her tongue.
She told the trees
in Seville her story. She was free
from the statues' fish eyes
until she remembered Lowry Loinseach
and his ass's ears. She heard her secret
whispered over the breakfast marmalade.
The women's smiles jack-knived,
their lips snapped closed
like purses. Now the oranges growing
along the sidewalks
reminded her of hospitals.
After the glorious mysteries,
the sorrowful.

Ceres in Caherlistrane

for Colum McCann

Somewhere near forty-second street.
a girl, copper-haired, sings for a hawk-eyed man.
He tastes, in the lark's pillar of sound
honey and turf-fires. A tinker's curse rings out:

This is the voice of Ireland, of what we were.
He approves. Her hair gleams. There is a vow.
Later, she skips into the grafitti-sprayed subway.
At the edge of hearing, a laugh, a man's death cry,

a woman's love call are carried out of the tunnel's
round mouth caught in the snatch of a tune.
She has no idea these underriver walls
are shored up with Irish bones, black men's bodies.

She thinks all the buskers in New York are down
here tonight like cats. She hears them – a keen,
a skein of blues. They speed her passage. She hums,
picking up the echoes in her river-run.

In Galway, her stooked hair ripens that Summer.
At Hallowe'en there are wineapples.* A seed caught
in her teeth will keep the cleft between this world
and the next open, the all souls' chorus a filter

for certain songs that rise from a cold source.
Brandy and honey notes replace spring water –
the gift price to sing an octave deeper
than sweet, tuned to a buried watercourse.

In the Name of God
and of the Dead Generations

I will tell you the sound the wounded make.
First let this be clear:
I always knew what belonged to me
the piece of ground under my feet
or my sleeping body was mine
and all the land between
an imaginary line fifteen feet
above the high water mark
and the shore at low tide
not including Manhattan
and in Spring, more,

* Wineapple is another name for the pomegranate.

which might be why Mediterranean
coastal regions pulled me
with their small tides;
or areas of high seismic activity
such as Lisbon and San Francisco –
so much for place. Yes
it has mattered, yes we replace
rock with the shimmering space,
an idea of a rock where the rock has been.

Yes, I understand abstraction.
It is the welcoming place
into which strangers may come,
people with gypsy blood and skin
darker again than that
of certain fishermen along the coast
but that all said I was born outside the pale
and am outside it still. I do not fit in.

Let me tell you the sound the wounded make.
Vowels that rise out of slashed throats
will be somewhat strangled
and inelegant in our Hiberno English.
The gurgled speech of Kosovo
ringed with hard Dublin argot
from the inner city
or drawn out by tender vowels in Clare
sounds uneducated as well as broken.
This is not sexy English,
not the accent to elicit
'Put a bit of butter on the spuds, Andre.'

There were new Jews in Brooklyn, new Irish
In the Bronx a hundred years ago –
their 'sweedhard' and 'stoah'
unbecoming in the mouths of young men
from Carna or Warsaw. These are the sounds
the wounded make.
An old man from the Gaeltacht* at a wedding
'Excuse me, miss, I don't speak English so good'
the Miss a branding iron.
In Irish the sentence would have sung.

* An area in which Irish is the first spoken language.

We have spent a small ransom
remembering the famine
that some of us never forgot
in universities all over America
and never gone looking for the ones that got away
from Mother Machree and the ancient order
of Hibernians, the black Irish.
They left in the darkened holds of coffin ships –
they arrive sealed in the holds of containers
wounded, sometimes dead, between the jigs and the reels
and the Céad Mile Faílte.*

* An expression of welcome.

The Poet's Lover Names her Price

The week of the Mission in nineteen fifty-nine
a man woke up just as a cat
big as a good-sized dog, sprang.
He was black as the pit of hell
and his eyes were on fire.
A miraculous medal saved the man in the end
but the struggle was terrible.
The smell of burning coal
on flesh and fur, lingered in the room for weeks.
'The claw marks are scrawbed* on my back,' he said.

He walks over the roofs
of your slip-slidy dreams.
It is not those modern demons
ineffectual in the light
you should heed –
your nights and your poems
are like suburbs. There is a price
on my love and a reward.

* Clawed, scratched.

Do something. Perform
a pious or religious act
to attract the big cat.
Grapple the truth from him.
It will take more
than a Latin act of contrition
to break his power
but I will give you an invocation.

Let him once break your stare
and his claws will sink in
to your throat and tear.
He will discard the heart,
it's the soul he's after.
If you win, he'll disappear
leaving the smell of scorched flesh
and a poem. Worth the mess.

The Cost of the Gift

He mortified the flesh, she pampered it. She mocked,
He shook his big head. She thought he was her bedrock.
When he moved, he took the ground out from under her.
That's how we believe it was because a woman

that loves with desperation goes mad when her house
breaks. The pain of those seams parting slowly between
roof and wall is more than she can bear this morning.
He strides away with his head in Ursa Major.

At home in the Universe, he's breathing free air.
She sees the house Gods leaving, like pets in his wake.
Sparks break off the stars and fly to his anvil chest,
ash settles on the sofa, on the children's beds.

When he pitches his tent out beyond Sirius
she's stuck in the house. In such a situation
one way or another, one often dies: People
take sides, the laws of mourning are not well observed.

What of him, recalled to a cold hearth, the beauty
evicted and his ribcage straining like roofbeams –
Did the household Gods sneak back like apalled children
and did he pet them absently because it was

not their fault? Neither the marble statues nor the
earthenware head. All speculation but two things:
his dark familiars, crow, jaguar, fox, though loosed, stayed;
from that day out, one eye, the hunter's, never slept.

After the Funeral, the Departure

The bags are badly packed. Is a last look allowed?
Before I leave I'll dust the lovely perfume flasks and wrap them
in a silk scarf like metaphors or torahs, storm green, chalice red
and a gold flecked cobalt I bought in Israel.

They have survived the rock splitting under the house,
the walls straining like weightlifters' arms, the noise.
I have seen objects as delicate in a New York museum,
a pretty Etruscan amphora beside some Spartan vases.

Time to roll up my sleeves, there is domestic work
waiting – knives to be sharpened, the house scoured, a grave
to be dug. Even if I am incompetent and hear the tough
women laughing at my efforts, see the disgust carved

into their faces as I sit with my forehead on the foot
of a sunken grave, let them be disgusted. I am disgusted myself.
I didn't see it boomeranging back to the weak spots until it hit –
the ga bolga* in the heart, the eye, the right breast.

All that remains is to let the wind read each face accurately –
to say goodbye lightly would be nice but I do not;
I move on reluctantly, like every daughter of history
who has left her father's house unwillingly or late.

* A harpoon-like javelin used by Cúchulainn.